WHEN YOU
PRAY

A PRACTICAL GUIDE TO AN
Orthodox Life of Prayer

L. Joseph Letendre

ANCIENT FAITH PUBLISHING

CHESTERTON, INDIANA

When You Pray: A Practical Guide to an Orthodox Life of Prayer
Copyright © 2017 L. Joseph Letendre

Published by:
  Ancient Faith Publishing
  A Division of Ancient Faith Ministries
  P.O. Box 748
  Chesterton, IN 46304

All Old Testament quotations, unless otherwise identified, are from the Orthodox Study Bible, © 2008 by St. Athanasius Academy of Orthodox Theology (published by Thomas Nelson, Inc., Nashville, Tennessee) and are used by permission. New Testament quotations are from the New King James Version of the Bible, © 1982 by Thomas Nelson, Inc., and are used by permission.

ISBN: 978-1-944967-23-9

Printed in the United States of America

25 24 23 22   16 15 14 13 12 11 10 9 8 7 6 5 4

This book is a distillation of several talks on prayer I was asked to give in early 2013. The first of these talks was given to the members of the St. Moses the Ethiopian Community, an Orthodox group at Indiana State Prison. It is to them that this work is dedicated.

> *I write for the unlearned about things in which I am unlearned myself . . . I write as one amateur to another.* —C. S. Lewis[1]

Contents

1   To Pray   7

2   Pray as You Can   13

3   Pray Attentively   17

4   Pray the Lord's Prayer   23

5   Pray the Psalms   27

6   Pray the Gospel   31

7   Pray for Others   35

8   Pray Frequently   41

9   Pray Faithfully   53

APPENDIX: What Monasticism Teaches Us   63

Notes   67

About the Author   71

1

To Pray

If we're at all serious about being Christians, serious about living in accordance with the gospel, we quickly realize that going to church is not enough. It requires what Fr. Alexander Schmemann called "the liturgy after the liturgy"—undertaken faithfully, daily, and obediently for a lifetime. The litmus test of faith is not what we do in church, but what we do after church. The list we are given is exhaustive and exhausting. In part, we are

✠ To acquire the mind of Christ (Phil. 2:5)

✠ To move from knowing about God to knowing God (1 Cor. 13:12)

✠ To love our enemies (Matt. 5:44)

✠ To forgive from the heart (Matt. 18:35)

☩ To resist having our lives shaped by the world around us (Rom. 12:2)

☩ To know joy in the midst of suffering (Phil. 4:4)

☩ To follow the commandments of the Gospel (John 14:15).

In turn, we are promised we will

☩ Be transformed by the renewing of our minds (Rom. 12:2)

☩ Become participants in the divine nature (2 Pet. 1:4)

☩ Know the love of Christ and be filled with all the fullness of God (Eph. 3:19)

☩ Cultivate the fruits of the Holy Spirit (Gal. 5:22–23)

☩ Become holy as God is holy (Lev. 11:44, et al.; 1 Pet. 1:16).

What makes all of this—both the undertaking and promised result—possible is God's grace. What makes grace accessible is prayer.

So, what is prayer? At its most basic, prayer is spending time with God—deliberately, explicitly, consciously spending time with God.

St. John Vianney, a nineteenth-century priest in rural France, noticed a farmer who would come into the church every morning and evening and just sit there with no Bible, no prayer book, no rosary. Finally, the saint asked the farmer what he was doing. "I look at Him," the farmer replied, "and He looks at me; and we are happy."

This is prayer.

To pray is to "come before [God's] face with thanksgiving" (Ps. 94/95:2). It is to "be still, and know" that God is the Lord (Ps. 45:11/46:10). Sometimes it is to be like Jacob, wrestling with an angel and refusing to let go until he blesses us (Gen. 32). And sometimes, frankly, it feels like futility, like echoing emptiness.

On the first pages of his book *Beginning to Pray,* Metropolitan Anthony Bloom warns:

> At the very onset there is, then, an important problem: the situation of one for whom God seems to be absent. . . . Obviously I am not speaking of a real absence—God is never really absent—but the *sense* of absence which we have. We stand before God and we shout into an empty sky, out of which there is no reply. We turn in all directions and He is not to be found.[2]

Prayer can be enduring this felt absence of God with faith, with hope, and with love.

Prayer, like any relationship, involves sacrifice, which elevates prayer to a sacramental act.

All sacraments, at their core, are acts of offering. Thus, in marriage, a couple offer their relationship. In the anointing of the sick, we offer our pain and suffering. In confession, it is our sins we place before Jesus. In the Eucharist, we offer our thanks to the Father, and we "offer ourselves, each other, and all our life" to Jesus, who has given all His life to us. Underlying every sacramental deed is the certainty that only what is freely offered in and through Christ to the Father may be filled and transformed by the Spirit.

Prayer is the way we place our day, our work, our relationships, our life, and our being on the altar, making them available to God to bless, sanctify, and, like the bread and wine of the Eucharist, transform into a means of communion with Him and with each other.

Anyone who prays, or has tried to pray and given up in discouragement, knows praying—really praying—is not easy. Praying consistently seems almost impossible. Too often and too easily, prayer becomes a burden: one more item on an already overcrowded to-do list. Failing to pray becomes a source of guilt and stress as we must once again admit our inconstancy and procrastination to our father confessor. Yet our Lord said, "Come to Me, all *you* who labor and are heavy laden, and I will give you rest. . . . For My yoke *is* easy and My burden is light" (Matt. 11:28–30).

The purpose of this book, then, is not to add to the burden but to ease it by distilling the advice and experience of those who pray. It comes down to this: To pray,

✠ pray as you can;

✠ pray attentively;

✠ pray the Lord's Prayer;

✠ pray the Psalms;

✠ pray the Gospels;

✠ pray for others;

✠ pray frequently;

✠ pray faithfully.

2

Pray as You Can

Pray as you can, not as you want.
—Fr. Thomas Hopko[3]

Beginning to pray, or beginning to pray anew, is like beginning an exercise program in January. Experienced weightlifters avoid the gym in the first two weeks of January. It is overcrowded, and the weights and machines are hogged by people who know neither what they're doing nor why. By the third week, most of them have gone, never to return.

One reason for this often-noted phenomenon is that people in the first flush of their New Year's resolutions try to do too much: too many sets, too many reps, dangerously heavy weights. The resulting pain, tedium, and failure prove to be powerful demotivators.

Something similar can happen with prayer. We set out determined to read so many prayers or so many psalms for a certain length of time, and it doesn't work. We soon give up, often for the same reason as the January gym enthusiasts: we try to do more than we can sustain. It is a combination of enthusiasm, naïvete, and pride—what my priest calls "mistaking adrenaline for the Holy Spirit."

No matter how many books about monks or monasticism we read, the fact is we cannot pray like monks unless we are monks. Mothers of young children must pray like mothers of young children. Factory managers with eight-hour jobs and two-hour commutes must pray like factory managers with eight-hour jobs and two-hour commutes.

How much time we can spend praying and when we can pray are determined by the circumstances of our lives as much as they are for monks and nuns, bishops and hermits. This can change from day to day. A mother who has stayed up all night nursing a sick child will not be able to pray much (if at all) when the time for morning prayer comes. But she need not worry; she has already kept an all-night vigil.

Prayer, like politics (and this is the only point of comparison), is the art of the possible. Coaches and physical trainers are often asked, "What is the best exercise? What's the best workout routine?" The correct answer is always the same: "The one you can stick with." The same holds for prayer.

In Bethany, two days before His Crucifixion, a woman came and anointed Jesus with costly perfume. The extravagant gesture is harshly criticized, but Jesus defends her act, saying, "She has done what she could" (Mark 14:8).

The decision to do what one can, however seemingly small or inadequate, recurs throughout the Bible: a young shepherd hurls stones at a giant warrior; out of a crowd of famished thousands, a boy graciously offers what few loaves he has; Peter tells a lame beggar, "Silver and gold I do not have, but what I do have I give you" (Acts 3:6). The giant falls, the thousands are fed, and the beggar leaps to his feet.

In prayer, all we need do is what we can.

3

Pray Attentively

Without attention there is no prayer.
—St. Ignatius Brianchaninov[4]

One of the first words of advice I received about prayer when I became Orthodox was a quotation from St. John of Kronstadt: "When praying, keep to the rule that it is better to say five words from the depth of your heart than ten thousand words with your tongue only."[5] It sounds fair. If I don't pay attention to my prayers, why should God?

Paying attention during prayer proved more difficult than I anticipated. My experience is not unique. Three highly recommended practices can help:

1. Preparing for prayer

2. Saying the words of our prayer slowly

3. Praying aloud

Recollection: Preparing to Pray

Before we can begin to pray, we must prepare to pray. We need to slow our thoughts, quiet our minds, and lower the voltage of our humming nerves, so that like the psalmist we can say, "My heart is ready, O God, my heart is ready" (Ps. 56:8/57:7).

In the Old Testament, a Sabbath was commanded for God's people on the seventh day, Saturday. No work was allowed for man or beast. Even the distance one could walk was strictly limited. To pray is to enter into a brief Sabbath. It is to accept, if only for an instant, Jesus' invitation: "Come to Me, all *you* who labor and are heavy laden, and I will give you rest" (Matt. 11:28).

If there is a school of Orthodox spirituality, it is hesychasm. The term comes from the Greek word *hesychia,* which means stillness, a coming to rest. Even if we are not monks using the hesychastic method, bringing ourselves as much as possible into a state of stillness and rest before we begin prayer is essential. If we don't, we will pray hastily and inattentively, then go rushing off to the next thing.

Few of us can practice attentive, deliberate prayer for even a minute unless we redirect our hearts, focus our will, and calm (or awaken) our minds. Western writers on prayer call this preparation "recollection." The term is apt. Recollection is the work of collecting our scattered attention, herding our wildly running thoughts.

It is an easily neglected part of prayer. Time is short; we have much to do besides. Like an athlete who won't warm up before training, we are impatient to begin the "real" praying.

How do we recollect ourselves? There are any number of ways:

- ✛ We can sit calmly, breathing deeply until our bodies relax and our minds quiet down.

- ✛ We can say the Jesus Prayer slowly for a few moments.

- ✛ We can remind ourselves that we are in the Presence of God.

- ✛ We can use our imagination to put ourselves in the place of someone in the Gospels: blind Bartimaeus crying to Jesus for mercy; the woman caught in adultery whose life has been spared; the disciples in Gethsemane, who can't stay awake.

✣ We can simply make it personal by recalling that we are not merely reciting or reading words by rote but addressing them to another person.

When we have calmed and quieted ourselves "like a weaned child with his mother" (Ps. 131:2 NKJV), or at least tried to, it is time to begin. But even if we can't recollect ourselves, we should begin anyway.

Pray Slowly

To pray attentively, we will have to force ourselves to pray slowly. We are opting for quality over quantity here: saying more prayers is not the same as praying better.

The way to say the words of our prayer is *slowly*. There must be no rushing. Our time is limited, but fortunately, it is better to say a few prayers slowly and attentively than to rush through many. Jesus tells us to avoid wordy prayers (Matt. 6:7). A few words said slowly, with as much attention as we can bring to bear on the words, are what is required. The list of people in the Gospels who have been healed, forgiven, or saved after the briefest of prayers is long. The wise thief, for instance, was saved after a mere nine words of prayer (Luke 23:42).

Pray Aloud

Praying aloud will help us pray attentively. By praying aloud, I do not mean shouting at the top of our voice. Writing teachers have their students read their papers aloud to themselves in a "twelve-inch voice." The person seated next to them should not be able to hear them; nonetheless, their lips are moving and their voices are engaged. This is what is meant by praying aloud: the words exhale from our lips and do not simply echo in our minds.

Praying aloud accomplishes the important function of slowing down our flow of words. We can think much faster than we speak. Forcing ourselves to say the words of our prayer aloud slows down our thoughts, and that makes it more likely we will pay attention to what we are saying.

The words of prayer—whether liturgical or personal—function as a two-edged sword. On one hand they are directed outward to God and are the medium of our praise and petition, repentance and thanksgiving. On the other hand, they are aimed inward at our own hearts and minds. They are meant to reshape our reflex response to the world around us and to bring our inclinations and decisions under the yoke of Christ. Praying aloud improves the accuracy of their aim.

Like prostrations and the sign of the cross, praying aloud incorporates our body. It makes us move our lips and tongues. Saying our prayers aloud engages our ears: we can hear what we are praying. As St. Paul reminds us, "faith comes by hearing" (Rom. 10:17). Praying with our body prevents our time of prayer from being reduced to thoughtful musings on religious themes or wallowing in pious sentiments. Something as simple as mouthing the words of prayer softly makes prayer effortful; it makes praying into work. It enlists the whole of our being.

4

Pray the Lord's Prayer

First and foremost, we pray the Lord's Prayer.

People sometimes ask about "praying in our own words." It is a curious turn of phrase: we never worry about talking in our own words.

I have grandchildren who are constantly talking to people in their own words. No one has any idea what they are saying. We call it babbling, and we know that soon it will become language others can understand. In order for communication to be possible, a vocabulary must be acquired and a host of phrases mastered. Parents help by prompting their children with "What do you say?" when a "please" or "thank you" is called for. In other words, a script is provided.

Prayer is no different. It requires language appropriate to the occasion. Otherwise, we become like

Peter on Mt. Tabor. The evangelists must hasten to excuse him: "he did not know what to say, for they were greatly afraid" (Mark 9:6). If we begin by praying in our own words, we will, at best, sound foolish. At worst, we may forget whom we are addressing and lapse into irreverence (like the woman who began a public prayer with "Lord, did You see the six o'clock news?").[6]

Praying from a script spares us the burden of originality. Originality is overrated—at least when it comes to prayer and theology. I've observed that in Christian theology the word "original" is invariably followed by the word "sin."

Without the right script, prayer can degenerate into telling God what He already knows, and then telling Him what we think He should do about it.[7]

When Jesus' disciples came to Him and asked, "Lord, teach us to pray," He responded by giving them a script: "When you pray, say: 'Our Father . . .'" (Luke 11:1, 2).

The earliest extrabiblical account of early Christian practice, the *Didache*,[8] is equally direct: "Do not pray like the hypocrites, but rather as the Lord commanded in the gospel: Our Father in heaven . . . Pray this three times each day" (8:2–3).

This is a nod to the psalmist's "evening and morning and midday" (Ps. 54:18/55:17). We find the same schedule faithfully adhered to by the Prophet Daniel, even at the risk of his own life: "Now when Daniel learned that the decree [forbidding prayer for thirty days] was posted, he entered his house, where the windows facing Jerusalem were open to him in the upper rooms, and he knelt down on his knees three times that day and prayed and gave thanks to his God, as he was doing before" (Dan. 6:11).

So, if you would pray, pray the Lord's Prayer three times daily (at least).

5

Pray the Psalms

The essential thing is for us to hear God's word and discover from it how to respond to him.

—Hans Urs von Balthasar[9]

The other script the Holy Spirit provides us is the Book of Psalms.

If prayer means intentionally spending time directing our attention to God, what happens when our attention flags? How do we keep our thoughts from wandering? How do we resist being swept along by the stream (or sewer) of consciousness? How do we fill (rather than kill) the time of prayer? For nearly three thousand years the answer has been: the Psalms.

The endorsement, by exhortation and example, of the Psalms as the text and teacher of prayer can be found in all the Christian centuries, in both East and West. In the twentieth century, prominent Western writers such as Dietrich Bonhoeffer, C. S. Lewis, Thomas Merton, and Eugene Peterson have all published books about praying the Psalms.

In one of these, *Psalms: The Prayerbook of the Bible,*[10] German pastor, theologian, and martyr Dietrich Bonhoeffer observes that the Lord's Prayer distills and concentrates everything in the Psalms. Conversely, the Psalms expand, elaborate, and apply every phrase in the Lord's Prayer. It's like the photos on our phones. With a flick of thumb and index finger, a photograph fills the screen; when we reverse the movement, the photograph shrinks back to a thumbnail. The Psalms and the Lord's Prayer function similarly: the Psalter expands the Lord's Prayer, and the Lord's Prayer summarizes the Psalms.

Putting It into Practice

How do we pray the Psalms? The Church's answer is: in order, repeatedly, continually. Start with Psalm 1:1: "Blessed is the man / Who walks not in the counsel of the ungodly, / Nor stands in the way of sinners, / Nor sits in the seat of the troublesome" and proceed, verse by verse, psalm by psalm, reading them in order until you come to the very last verse: "Let everything that breathes praise the Lord. / Alleluia."

Then go back to Psalm 1 and do it again.

And again.

Continue this for the rest of your life.

In *The Grace of Incorruption*, Dartmouth English professor Donald Sheehan wrote, "Since September 8, 1984, when I was received into the Orthodox Church, I have prayed the Psalms daily in my morning and evening private prayer; and since May, 1988, when I was ordained to the subdiaconate, I have prayed through the entire Psalter every week of my life."[11]

How should we pray the Psalms?

✠ **Aloud.** The dance of tongue, teeth, and lips is part of prayer. In *The Arena*, St. Ignatius Brianchaninov writes, "Say the words in an audible voice when you are alone: this also helps hold the attention."[12]

✠ **Slowly and attentively.** What St. Ignatius Brianchaninov says of the Jesus Prayer (more on this below) applies to psalmic prayer: "The essential properties of this prayer should be: attention, the enclosure of the mind in the words of prayer, extreme unhurriedness in pronouncing it, and contrition of heart . . . these conditions are necessary for all prayer."[13]

How many psalms should we pray?

Monks and nuns are the Church's experts in psalmic prayer. In monasteries and sketes that are able to follow the monastic rule fully, the entire Psalter—all 150 psalms—is read every week. This increases to twice a week during Great Lent. To facilitate this, centuries ago, the Psalms were divided into twenty sections (called *kathismas*) and further divided into three subsections (called *stases*): thus, sixty sections of roughly equal length. So, one possibility is to pray one or more of these stases each day.[14]

Here we must again remember first principles: Pray as you can, not as you want; do fewer things better. If praying a stasis attentively is not possible, do less. Do one psalm. Do a few verses from one psalm. We should pray as many—or as few—psalms as we realistically can in the time we have. But we should never do none.

6

Pray the Gospel

The next ingredient in prayer is the prayerful reading of the Bible. Not just any kind of reading, but a very specific kind of reading.

Generally speaking, there are three ways to read Scripture.

First, there is what could be termed a "broad" reading of the Bible. Here the purpose is to become biblically literate. We should know the stories; we should have a general familiarity with biblical events and characters (and some of them really were characters). In times past, this was expected of any educated person, even if that person was not a regular churchgoer or even a believer.

We should easily recall the basic principles of living the Christian life, and these should shape our character, inform our conscience, and guide our day-to-day decisions. Some verses (if not word-for-word quotations, at least close paraphrases) should leap into our minds when needed. This broad reading should be part of the daily practice of any Christian. (My priest says we should do one hour of Bible reading for every hour we spend watching television.)

The second kind of reading is Bible study. Rather than aiming at general familiarity, we take a narrower and more specific focus. We are seeking greater depth and detail. We may look more deeply at one book or one author, or follow one idea through the entire Scripture. Tools like Orthodox study Bibles, commentaries, and concordances can help. This can be done by ourselves, with a small group, or in a more formal class, and usually it will not be done daily.

The goal of these two types of reading is familiarity, knowledge, deeper understanding, and, ultimately, living scripturally. In Edmund Rostand's play, *Cyrano de Bergerac*, Cyrano's nemesis asks him, by way of warning, "Have you ever read *Don Quixote?*"

"Read it?" Cyrano replies. "I've lived it!"

That is the goal of Bible reading and Bible study. While both of these types of reading should be undertaken prayerfully, they are not, in the strictest sense, prayer.

The third way of reading Scripture *is* prayer. It goes by several names: "meditation" and "spiritual reading" are commonly used. For convenience, I will use the Latin term *lectio divina*: "sacred reading."

The example for this kind of reading, as for so much in the spiritual life, is found in Mary, the Mother of our Lord. Twice in his Gospel, St. Luke describes her as pondering things "in her heart" (Luke 2:19, 51). This is precisely what lectio divina involves: pondering the Word of God in our hearts.

With lectio the aim is not simply knowledge of and obedience to God's word, it is communion with God.

How is it done?

First, choose a *short* passage from the Gospels. It can be one event in the life of Christ, a section from the teachings of Jesus, even a single verse. The guiding principle here, again, is "do fewer things better." Even one verse can be enough. In St. Athanasius's *Life of St. Anthony*, we read how hearing just one verse from the Gospel in Church led Anthony into the desert to pursue the monastic life.

Second, read the passage or verse out loud—again, "faith comes by hearing" (Rom. 10:17). Read it slowly. Then read it again. For writers across the centuries, the governing image here is "ruminating." A ruminant (cows are the handiest example) is an animal that chews its cud. After it has eaten, it regurgitates its food and spends its time in a leisurely rechewing of its meal. When the saints advise ruminating on a passage of Scripture, they mean slowly "chewing over" what we've read in our minds and our imagination.

Three things to keep in mind when practicing lectio:

1. Do not question the Bible; let the Bible question you.

2. Do not worry about what you do not understand; worry about what you do understand. An honest confusion is better than a false clarity.

3. Remember that the goal of this reading is for you to be listening attentively to God through His Word.

The everyday work of loving someone means, in large part, paying attention to them and listening to them. Loving God "with all your heart, with all your soul, and with all your strength" (Deut. 6:5 NKJV) is no different. It involves listening to His word in the Bible. As God Himself commands: "This is My beloved Son, in whom I am well pleased. Hear Him!" (Matt. 17:5).

7

Pray for Others

If we pray, we will want to pray for others. This is often called intercessory prayer.

As always, it is helpful to pray as the Church prays. The intercessory prayers in the anaphoras of Saints John Chrysostom and Basil provide us a model. If we read them, several things stand out.

Remembrance

Like the Psalms, the liturgy provides a script for prayer. The key word is "remember." When we pray for others, we begin by asking God to remember those we are remembering. Each petition in the anaphoras begins with, "Remember, O Lord." Using St. Basil's words, for instance, the Church asks God to "Remember, O Lord, those in prison and all who suffer . . . those who have fallen asleep before us in the hope of eternal life . . . those who have asked us to pray for them," and so forth.

So with us. We ask God to remember those whom we remember and (just in case) anyone we've forgotten.

The List

When praying for others, the Church makes use of a simple tool: a list of names. We can do the same.

A list of names is powerful. The Vietnam War Memorial in Washington, DC, is simply a chronologically ordered list of the names of all who died in the war. Over 58,000 names are carved into slabs of black rock. Every day, people come to leave pictures and flowers, look for the names of people they knew, or just read some of the names. Some weep. It has been called "the Wall that heals."

To pray for others, we need only maintain written lists of the names of those for whom we want to pray. During our time of prayer we read them unhurriedly before God, beginning with the prayer, "Remember, O Lord." (Of course, no written list is needed for those names written on our hearts.)

Our lists can include the names of everyone included in our parish directory. Teachers may list all the students they have taught, grouped by the year they graduated; doctors, nurses, and therapists may pray for their patients; we may pray for our co-workers. The list should include those we have hurt and, more importantly, those who have hurt us. If the list is long (and it will be) or time is short (as it usually is), we will not be able to pray through our entire list. Instead, we will pray through a portion of the list, perhaps ending with a line from St. Basil's Liturgy: "Remember those I have forgotten because of the multitude of names. Remember them, for you know the names and needs of each."

When we have completed our list, we move on—in trust and confidence—to the rest of our prayer, the rest of our day, or simply to our rest. It is not our prayer or the intensity of feeling we bring to it that matters; what matters is God's grace. Through our prayers we have joined in the work God is already doing; we have united God's will for them to our own.

The Request

When we remember a person or a group of people, we often remember their needs. Phrases like, "who is ill, who is looking for work, who is preparing for marriage" will be part of our remembrance.

In St. Basil's Liturgy, we read a breathless cascade of requests he makes for his people:

> Fill their treasuries with every good thing;
> preserve their marriages in peace and harmony;
> raise the infants; guide the young; support
> the faint-hearted; reunite the separated; lead
> back those in error and unite them to your
> holy, catholic and apostolic Church; free
> those who are held captive by unclean spir-
> its; travel with those who travel; defend the
> widows; protect the orphans; heal the sick.

In many cases, the need is obvious and can be expressed in few words: healing for the sick, strength for the burdened, comfort for the grieving, mercy for the departed, justice for the oppressed, wisdom for our leaders, guidance for the confused. In other cases, the all-inclusive prayer for mercy will be enough.

We can finish with a general prayer. Perhaps we will end with a verse from a psalm or the last, summary petition of the Great Litany: "Help them, save them, have mercy on them, and protect them, O God, by your grace."

One caveat: If we pray for others, we are volunteering to help. This point is movingly illustrated in the musical based on Victor Hugo's novel, *Les Miserables*. The protagonist, Jean Valjean, is trying to help a student named Marius. Marius and his companions are trapped after a failed attempt to start a revolution. As they wait behind their barricades for the sunrise attack that will end their lives, Valjean prays for Marius that God will bring him home. When the attack comes, it is Valjean who brings him home, carrying the wounded Marius on his back through the Paris sewers to safety.

The word "intercede" means to "intervene," "to step in between." This is what Moses most memorably did:

> Therefore He said that He would destroy them,
> Had not Moses His chosen one stood before
>   Him in the breach,
> To turn away His wrath, lest He destroy them.
> (Ps. 106:23 NKJV)

Praying for others can be risky. The risk is that we will become part of God's answer to our prayer. We should be ready for that.

8

Pray Frequently

In order to become eventually capable of unceasing prayer [we] must practice frequent prayer.

— St. Ignatius Brianchaninov[15]

Prayer should be made frequently. . . but briefly.

— St. John Cassian[16]

Practically every Orthodox book on prayer quotes St. Paul's admonition to "pray without ceasing" (1 Thess. 5:17). In the Orthodox Church, entire schools and disciplines of prayer have developed to help people acquire this grace. The five-volume anthology on prayer, *The Philokalia*, was collected primarily to give guidance and instruction in the practice of ceaseless prayer.

Few of us living "in the world"—meaning outside of monasteries—can pray without ceasing. Work-day distractions and obligations, many of them part of our vocations, eat away at our time and attention. But even if we cannot pray ceaselessly, we can pray frequently. We can seize every opportunity the day affords us to pray briefly; we can pray on the run.

Indeed, frequent prayer is essential if we are to grow in the Christian life and fulfill the command-ments of Christ. Without frequent prayer, living the Christian life is all but impossible. As Jesus warned us, "Without Me you can do nothing" (John 15:5). Therefore, besides praying at the set times of our rule, we should make every event, activity, and tran-sition in our day an opportunity for a brief prayer.

"When you pray," Jesus instructs His disciples, "do not use vain repetitions as the heathen *do*. For they think that they will be heard for their many words. Therefore do not be like them" (Matt. 6:7–8).

In *Jesus Through Middle Eastern Eyes*[17] Ken Bailey gives context to Jesus' warning. In the world of the Roman Empire, citizens petitioning a government official would begin by addressing them with an effu-sive flood of titles and flatteries that to our modern ears sound tedious and ridiculous. (Unhappy is the lot of the Latin student who must translate these.) Jesus dismisses all of that. We are not addressing a powerful imperial official in the hopes of gaining a favor; we are addressing a Father who loves us.

The rule, then, for this kind of prayer is: Keep it simple. Keep it short.

To increase the frequency of our prayers, here are four "methods" (for want of a better term) that have seen wide use.

Grace Before Everything

"Saying grace" is shorthand for the practice of offering a brief prayer of thanks and blessing before eating a meal. Prolific British writer G. K. Chesterton says we shouldn't stop there. "You say grace before meals. All right. But I say grace before the concert and the opera, and grace before the play and pantomime, and grace before I open a book, and grace before sketching, painting, swimming, fencing, boxing, walking, playing, dancing, and grace before I dip the pen in the ink."[18]

Chesterton's list can be lengthened indefinitely. Not only should we say grace before we eat, but grace before we cook and before we wash the dishes. We can give thanks when we are confronted with anything that gives us joy and delight: the laughter of a child, sunlight streaming through the clouds, finding a parking space . . . The importance of constantly giving thanks to God cannot be overstressed. In the Epistle to the Colossians, St. Paul describes what could be termed the "Christian lifestyle":

> Be thankful. Let the word of Christ dwell
> in you richly in all wisdom, teaching and
> admonishing one another in psalms and
> hymns and spiritual songs, singing with
> grace in your hearts to the Lord. And what-
> ever you do in word or deed, *do* all in the
> name of the Lord Jesus, giving thanks to
> God the Father through Him. (3:15–17)

Three times in these two verses St. Paul urges his listeners to give thanks. Elsewhere, in what scholars believe was his first epistle, he tells the Thessalonians "in everything give thanks; for this is the will of God in Christ Jesus for you" (1 Thess. 5:18). Christian philosopher Joseph Pieper reminds us:

> We have only to think for a moment how
> much of the Christian understanding of life
> depends upon belief in Grace; to think that

the Holy Spirit is in a special sense a gift; . . .
that everything gained and everything claimed
follows upon something given, and comes
after something gratuitous and unearned;
that in the beginning there is always a gift.[19]

If there is always a gift, there is always a Giver, and
so there must also always be the giving of thanks. It
is no accident that the pivotal act of Christian worship is called the Eucharist—a Greek word that translates simply as "thanksgiving." The Eucharist is not
only the center of the Church's worship, it is meant
to be the axis of our personal prayer and to set the
tone for the whole of our life. Thus, in his last sermon, preached on Thanksgiving Day in 1983, Fr.
Alexander Schmemann famously began by declaring,
"Everyone capable of thanksgiving is capable of sal-
vation and eternal joy."

Practicing the Presence of God

Another way of increasing the frequency of our
prayers is described in the classic spiritual book *The
Practice of the Presence of God*. This way is simply to
maintain a running conversation with God throughout our day.

In this book, a Catholic priest named Joseph de

Beaufort provides us letters and a record of conversa-
tions with Brother Lawrence, a Carmelite monk living in seventeenth-century Paris who worked in the
monastery kitchen until his death in 1691.

Brother Lawrence said we could "be constantly
aware of God's presence, continually talking to him
throughout each day." He added that it is not too difficult. "In the beginning . . . a little effort was needed
to form the habit of continuously conversing with
God, telling Him everything that was happening.
However, after a little careful practice, God's love
refreshed him and it became quite easy."[20]

A striking example of this type of prayer can be
found in Terrence Malick's 2011 film *The Tree of Life*.
Writer Peter Leithart remarks that he has "never
seen a film so drenched in prayer as *The Tree of Life*.
During the film's first half hour, there is more prayer
than dialogue."[21]

Most of the prayers we overhear belong to Mrs.
O'Brien, the mother of the film's central character.
The film begins by contrasting two ways of living:
the way of nature and the way of grace. While still a
child, Mrs. O'Brien chose to follow the way of grace,
promising in one prayer, "I will be true to You whatever comes."

Years later, when she learns her nineteen-year-old

son has died, her prayers become more poignant and pointed:

"My hope. My God.

"Was I false to You? Lord, why? Where were You? Did You know?

"What are we to You? Answer me."

Prayer also finds its way into Malick's next film, *To the Wonder*. At one point the character Marina prays, "Love who love us, thank you."

For those of us whose days are filled with crowded hours and for whom the steps discussed above—recollection, psalmody, leisurely and thoughtful Bible reading—are impossible, after a brief grounding in prayer (a line from a psalm, the Our Father, a short verse or two from the Gospels), practicing the presence will be the path of prayer.

Short and Simple

One simple way to "practice the presence" is to have a short, simple prayer we can use at any time, any place, and in any circumstance.

For this kind of prayer, our script can come from a psalm verse or a line from the liturgy. For example, during the Presanctified Liturgy of the fifth week of Great Lent, the verses on "Lord, I Call" are greatly multiplied. Once they exceed the number of psalm verses, the refrain for all the extra verses is "Before I perish utterly, save me, O Lord."

In the early Church, the great witness to this type of prayer is St. John Cassian. In his *Conferences*, he records that for praying constantly, the prayer of choice among the monks was the verse "O God, make haste to help me" (Ps. 69:2/70:1). In one chapter he transcribes the words of Abba Isaac, who goes into great detail about how this psalm verse serves as the prayer for all times and situations: when struggling with weariness, weakness, or distraction; when facing temptation or danger; in times of doubt, despair, or confusion:

> This, then, is the devotional formula proposed
> to you as absolutely necessary for possessing
> the perpetual awareness of God: "O God,
> incline unto my aid; O Lord, make haste to
> help me." Not without reason has this verse
> been taken from out of the whole body of
> Scripture. For it takes up all the emotions
> that can be applied to human nature and
> with great correctness and accuracy it adjusts
> itself to every condition and every attack.[22]

The Jesus Prayer

Of course, the best known and most widely used short prayer in the Orthodox Church is the Jesus Prayer. In many ways, it has become the cornerstone of Orthodox spirituality. It is the tool *par excellence* for attaining the habit of ceaseless prayer. An entire school of spirituality—hesychasm—is built on it. Volumes have been written by the saints to guide those using it—most notably the five-volume *Philokalia* and, more recently, Abbot Chariton of Valaamo's anthology *The Art of Prayer*.[23] Few books on prayer fail to mention the Jesus Prayer.

Variations exist, but the usual wording of the prayer is "Lord Jesus Christ, Son of God, have mercy on me, a sinner." It is important to remember that this is a prayer like any other. It is not a magical incantation that must be said "just right" to have an effect. The prayer can be shortened. The prayer can be adapted to the liturgical year or to our needs: "Lord Jesus Christ, who is risen from the dead, have mercy on me." "Lord Jesus Christ, Son of God, heal me." The authors agree that what is essential is the invocation of the holy name of Jesus—that and the prayer's deep roots in Scripture.

Lord Jesus Christ—the name through which all

"shall be saved" (Rom. 10:13) and at which "every knee should bow, of those in heaven, and of those on earth, and of those under the earth, and *that* every tongue should confess that Jesus Christ *is* Lord, to the glory of God the Father" (Phil. 2:10–11).

Son of God—"Whoever confesses that Jesus is the Son of God, God abides in him, and he in God" (1 John 4:15).

Have mercy on me—the answered prayer of blind Bartimaeus, "Jesus, Son of David, have mercy on me" (Mark 10:47), and the publican's justifying "God, be merciful to me a sinner" (Luke 18:13).

A sinner—"If we confess our sins, He is faithful and just to forgive us *our* sins and to cleanse us from all unrighteousness" (1 John 1:9).

The word "mercy" translates the Greek word *eleison,* which means "oil." In the Mediterranean world, oil was more than simply an ingredient in cooking. Oil fueled the lamps that dispelled the darkness and was medicine used for healing. The Good Samaritan applied first aid to the man who had fallen among thieves by pouring wine and oil on the man's wounds (Luke 10:34). To ask God for mercy, then, is to ask not only for the forgiveness of our sins but for healing, enlightenment, and nourishment.

Some forms of the prayer leave out "a sinner." I

think it better to keep it. When the Pharisees criticized Jesus' choice of dinner companions, He replied, "I have not come to call *the* righteous, but sinners" (Luke 5:32). We can number ourselves among those He has called. Furthermore, a whole range of problems can be prevented. Some of the worst things Christians have done, the most shameful episodes in church history, occurred when members of the Church forgot that they, too, were sinners.

In the movie *Amazing Grace,* there is a powerful moment when John Newton, the ex-slave ship captain who wrote "Amazing Grace," is dictating his memoirs. Newton laments that he has forgotten so much, but he says, "Although my memory is fading, there are two things I remember clearly: I am a great sinner, and Christ is a great Savior."

If we remind ourselves often that we, too, are sinners, we will be less likely to judge, more likely to forgive, and more willing to pray.

9

Pray Faithfully

Consistently going to the gym and lifting weights will make you stronger—whether you enjoy your workouts or not. Prayer is like that. To pray well and reap its graces, we must pray faithfully. This requires persistence and perseverance. Few things in life are as difficult as sustaining a "long obedience in the same direction."[24]

Persistence in prayer is something Jesus repeatedly encourages in the Gospels.

In the Sermon on the Mount, our Lord issues His invitation to prayer: "Ask, and it will be given to you; seek, and you will find; knock, and it will be opened to you" (Matt. 7:7). In the original Greek, the verbs translated *ask, seek,* and *knock* are in a tense that commands ongoing action, not a one-time occurrence. A more accurate translation might be "keep asking . . . keep seeking . . . keep knocking." Don't ever stop.

In the Gospel of Luke, after teaching the Our Father, Jesus presents the parable of the persistent friend. A man is awoken from a sound sleep at midnight by a friend who needs bread to feed a late-arriving guest. The man doesn't want to get up, "yet because of [his friend's] persistence he will rise and give him as many as he needs" (Luke 11:8).[25]

Later on in Luke, Jesus tells another parable to the effect that "men always ought to pray and not lose heart" (18:1). A persistent widow will give a judge no peace until he gives her justice against an adversary. In the end, the judge relents: "Though I do not fear God nor regard man, yet because this widow troubles me I will avenge her, lest by her continual coming she weary me" (Luke 18:4–5).

By Rule

Establishing a rule of prayer is key to staying faithful. Tell yourself, "I can pray anytime," and you end up never praying. If we are commanded to pray at all times, we must at least pray sometime. There must be points in our day when we interrupt all other activity to pray. In order to manage this ascetic feat, a rule of prayer is vital.

The word "rule" derives from the Latin word *regula*, which is also the root of our word "regular." To pray faithfully means to pray regularly. Establishing a rule means we are determined our praying will not be at the whim of how energetic or tired we feel, the mood we're in, or what's on television.

Establishing a rule of prayer simply means setting a time for prayer and deciding what we will do during that time. Monastic rules do this for monastic communities, specifying when the community will gather for prayer, what psalms will be chanted, and how this will be adjusted to different days and seasons. We must do the same. It is helpful to do this in consultation with another person—a priest or someone who knows us and has experience in prayer.

To do this, we first need to answer certain questions: Given our schedule, obligations, health, and so on, at what time can we pray? How long can we take? How many psalms and how much scripture can we read attentively in that length of time? What prayer-book prayers do we want to incorporate?

This appointment with God must be adhered to strictly. Sometimes we'll have to shorten it, but we should never abandon it entirely. Prayer, like any exercise, requires consistency if it is to bear fruit.

Faith and Feeling

More than our busy lives, more than disruptions and interruptions, more than asteroid strikes or the zombie apocalypse, the great enemy of consistent prayer is our constantly shifting feelings about the whole effort.

Since we live in a time when faith has been sentimentalized and romanticized, we need to consider the role of feelings in prayer. If one looks at the human trinity of thought, feeling, and action, spirituality (for want of a better word) is seen largely as a matter of feeling, separated from thought and only indirectly involved with action. It has become primarily a way to cultivate specific feelings: feelings of inner peace and serenity, connectedness, mindfulness, or whatever the current buzzword is. This is not the point of prayer.

The danger lies in equating prayer, or the quality of our prayer, with certain feelings. In *The Screwtape Letters,* C. S. Lewis's demon lets his protegé Wormwood in on the trick of using feelings to sabotage prayer:

Keep them watching their own minds and
trying to produce feelings there by the action of

their own wills. When they meant to ask Him for charity, let them, instead, start trying to manufacture charitable feelings for themselves and not notice that this is what they are doing. When they meant to pray for courage, let them really be trying to feel brave. . . . Teach them to estimate the value of each prayer by their success in producing the desired feeling; and never let them suspect how much success or failure of that kind depends on whether they are well or ill, fresh or tired, at the moment.[26]

Remember: we have not been commanded to feel grateful; we have been commanded to give thanks—whether we feel grateful or not.

Prayer is an offering, not a purchase. One of the things that distinguishes prayer from the pursuit of warm and fuzzy spiritual experiences is that, far from making us feel better, prayer can make us feel worse.

If we pray faithfully, we come to see our sins more clearly, both their roots in ourselves and their fruits in the world. Just as it is easier to see the dust and cobwebs in a well-lit room, so it is easier to see our sins when we pray. The growing awareness of our sinfulness is a sign that we are praying to the real God and not to an idol of our own imagining. Unlike the real God, an idol will never disagree with us.

The fact of the matter is that, if we pray, most of the time most of us will feel nothing. In 2007, the letters of St. Teresa of Calcutta were published.[27] One reviewer remarked, "Most of its pages reveal not the serene meditations of a Catholic sister confident in her belief, but the agonized words of a person confronting a terrifying period of darkness that lasted for decades."[28] Secular reviewers were surprised; Christians who pray were not. These "dark nights" (a term that comes from the writings of St. John of the Cross) or "periods of dryness" are normal and should be expected. This is the reason the first chapter of Metropolitan Anthony Bloom's book *Beginning to Pray* is entitled "The Absence of God."

This phenomenon is consistent with the biblical experience of God. In the ziggurats and high places of the pagan tribes who surrounded God's people, the centerpiece of every temple was the large statue of a god. The Parthenon of Athens housed a forty-foot gold and ivory statue of Athena. To the ancients, Solomon's temple in Jerusalem would have been a startling contrast: the Holy of Holies held, not an imposing, richly adorned statue, but rather an empty seat. The center of the covenant life of God's people was, in fact, an absence that revealed a presence.

We find the same thing in the New Testament: Early in the morning on the first day of the week, the women come to the tomb of Jesus only to find that the stone has been rolled away and the tomb is empty. Before they meet the risen Christ, they first face His absence.

Periods of dryness can be periods of purification. It is possible to make an idol of our own praying. Is it some "spiritual experience" or serene feeling we are seeking in prayer, or is God our goal? Is it communion with God and the keeping of the Gospel commandments? In periods of dryness, God may be asking, "Is it Me you love, is it Me you are seeking? Or is it just the way you feel in My presence?"

Sometimes prayer is like going to the dentist. When serious work is required, the dentist injects Novocain into our gums so we feel nothing during the procedure. When we feel nothing during prayer, it could be that the deep healing has begun.

This is the point where the act of prayer becomes a work of faith. We come to our chosen time, place, and rule of prayer. We are reluctant, procrastinating, distracted, and restless. We feel nothing, if not a little foolish. Nonetheless, we pray. The Latin word for "faith" is *credo*, the source of our word "credit." At heart, it means "trust." To pray during the dry times is to trust that the emptiness within and the absence without constitute, in fact, a presence. To pray a few words while frantically running from task to task is to trust that God hears us even if we can't hear Him. To have faith also means to act as if—as if God is real, as if God is there.

When we do this, from time to time we feel God's presence. Orthodox philosopher and diplomat Charles Malik observed, "those who know [Christ] and love him and trust him and seek his presence day and night are granted, at his pleasure, his Holy Spirit who guides them into all truth."[29] During prayer, we will, from time to time, gain insight or feel peace and a quiet joy not manufactured by our own efforts. It is not the result of using the right techniques, the way the right diet and exercise will reshape our bodies. It is grace and gift: hoped for yet unexpected; sought yet surprising.

Nonetheless, the test of prayer is not how we feel or what happens during prayer; it is what we do and how we are after prayer. A friend of mine once observed that her brother had begun meditating and jogging. "He is calmer and thinner," she remarked, "but he's no better." The fruits of prayer are revealed in the kitchen, the supermarket, and the office. This is why in the prophetic literature of the Old Testament we often read that God does not judge His people on the basis of their prayers, fasts, and ritual sacrifices in the temple, but on how they treat the widow, the fatherless, and the stranger (Zech. 7:10, for instance).

The test of prayer is how well we fulfill the commandments of Christ. St. Ignatius Brianchaninov reminds us of God's promise that "the person who fulfills the commandments of the Gospel will not only be saved but will enter into the most intimate union with God and become a divinely built temple of God."[30] The fruits of prayer are also the fruits of the Holy Spirit: love, joy, peace, patience, kindness, goodness, faithfulness, gentleness, and self-control (Gal. 5:22–23).

No wonder, then, that St. Theophan the Recluse reminds us, "If you are not successful in your prayer, do not expect success in anything. [Prayer] is the root of all."[31]

So, when you pray:

✚ Pray as you can

✚ Pray attentively

✚ Pray the Lord's Prayer

✚ Pray the Psalms

✚ Pray the Gospels

✠ Pray for others

✠ Pray frequently

✠ Pray faithfully.

And then: Arise, take up your cross, and follow Christ.[32]

APPENDIX

What Monasticism Teaches Us

The two sources Orthodox Christians rely on most for instruction in prayer are, first, the Bible, and then the writings of the monastic Fathers. Their teachings can be broadly summarized in the following six principles:

1. Rule
Set up basic routines and a schedule for your life that you rarely deviate from. Within your schedule, make time for prayer, Scripture reading, and periods of silence.

2. Spiritual Direction
Routinely meet with an older Christian (often it will be your priest) to talk about your life. This is not the same as counseling, therapy, or confession.

3. Obedience
One of the three traditional monastic vows is obedience. For those "in the world" it means accepting cheerfully and living up to the obligations imposed

by the circumstances of your life: where you live, your family, your work or school, the people you interact with, and so on.

4. Poverty

Poverty is another of the monastic vows. It challenges us to learn the difference between what we need and what we want, what we really want and what we're being programmed to want by advertisers and marketers. It calls us to be good stewards of our money and of our time, energy, talent, and attention. Avoid "affluenza." Give generously, even sacrificially.

5. Vigilance

Always be on your guard. Watch what you let yourself think about or imagine. Be careful what you watch, listen to, or look at. Exercise caution, especially with the entertainment you choose.

6. Prayer

The Four Cornerstones of Prayer:

Liturgy

✠ Attend as many services as possible

✠ Receive the sacraments frequently

✠ Keep the fasts and celebrate the feasts

The Hours

✢ Psalms and the Our Father

✢ Three times a day—more, if possible

✢ Done at set times of the day

✢ Shorten if unavoidable, but never eliminate

The Jesus Prayer

✢ Use a short, easily repeated prayer

✢ Use the Jesus Prayer or a psalm verse

✢ Intermix with the psalms

✢ Use when you don't have anything you need to think about or pay attention to (e.g. in the checkout line)

Spiritual Reading

✢ Short, prayerful reading of the Scripture, Fathers, etc.

✢ Think about it, then pray

✢ Take something with you from the reading: something to do, a word or verse to repeat to yourself during the day

Notes

1. Lewis, C. S., *Reflections on the Psalms* (New Work: Harcourt, Brace & Co., 1958), pp. 1–2.
2. Bloom, Anthony, *Beginning to Pray* (Mahwah, NJ: Paulist Press, 1970), p. 26.
3. I first read this in *The Spiritual Letters of John Chapman*, formulated as, "Pray as you can, not as you can't." It has been reiterated by Fr. Thomas Hopko in his "55 Maxims for the spiritual life."
4. Brianchaninov, St. Ignatius, *The Arena* (Jordan-ville, NY: Holy Trinity Monastery, 1997), p. 85.
5. St. John of Kronstadt, *My Life in Christ.*
6. Witnessed and related by Fr. Thomas Hopko.
7. Fr. Alexander Schmemann, quoting his teacher Archimandrite Cyprian Kern.
8. Also known as "The Teaching of the Apostles." Patristic scholars generally agree that some parts of the *Didache* date as early as the 80s. In other words, they were written at roughly the same time as the Gospels of St. Matthew and St. Luke.

9. von Balthasar, Hans Urs, *Prayer* (San Francisco: Ignatius Press, 1986), p. 15.

10. Bonhoeffer, Dietrich, *Psalms: The Prayerbook of the Bible* (Minneapolis: Augsburg Publishing House, 1970), p. 16.

11. Sheehan, Donald, *The Grace of Incorruption* (Brewster, MA: Paraclete Press, 2015), p. 153.

12. *The Arena,* p. 70.

13. *The Arena,* p. 78.

14. The word *kathisma* means "sitting," and *stasis* means "standing." Apparently, the monastic practice was to sit for the Psalms and then stand for the doxology at the end of each section.

15. *The Arena,* p. 83.

16. Died in 435. Also known as John the Roman, he toured the East visiting the second generation of monks in the Egyptian desert and elsewhere. He also served as a deacon to St. John Chrysostom in Constantinople. "Conference of Abba Isaac," p. 36, *The Conferences* (New York: Newman Press, 1997), p. 353.

17. Bailey, Kenneth, *Jesus Through Middle Eastern Eyes* (Downers Grove, IL: IVP Academic, 2008), pp. 92–94.

18. Early Notebook, Mid 1890s—*Collected Works of G. K. Chesterton: Collected Poetry* (San Franciso: Ignatius Press, 1994), p. 43.

19. Pieper, Joseph, *Leisure: The Basis of Culture* (Indianapolis: Liberty Fund, 1998), p. 17.

20. Brother Lawrence, *The Practice of the Presence of God* (New Kensington, PA: Whitaker House, 1982), pp. 3, 7.

21. Leithart, Peter J., *Shining Glory: Theological Reflections on Terrence Malick's Tree of Life* (Eugene, OR: Cascade Books, 2013), p. 28.

22. Cassian, John, *The Conferences*, p. 379.

23. Abbot Chariton, *The Art of Prayer* (London: Faber & Faber, 1966).

24. Friedrich Nietzsche, used by Eugene H. Peterson as the title for his book on the Psalms of Ascent (Downers Grove, IL: IVP Books, 2000). These fifteen psalms are chanted at the Liturgy of the Presanctified Gifts.

25. The Greek word *anaideia*, here translated as "persistence," is also rendered as "audacity" and "importunity" in other translations.

26. Lewis, C. S., *The Screwtape Letters* (New York: HarperCollins, 2001), p. 16.

27. Mother Teresa, *Come Be My Light* (New York: Doubleday, 2007).

28. Martin, James, "A Saint's Dark Night," *The New York Times*, August 29, 2007.

29. Malik, Charles Habib, *A Christian Critique of the University* (Waterloo, ON: North Waterloo Academic Press, 1982), p. 23.

30. *The Arena*, p. 2.

31. *The Art of Prayer*, p. 74.

32. Mark 2:11; 8:34.

About the Author

L. Joseph Letendre is the author of the popular guide *Preparing for Confession*. His writing has also appeared in *Touchstone, The Reformation and Revival Journal,* and *St. Vladimir's Theological Quarterly*. He recorded the audiobook of St. Nicholai Velimirovic's *Prayers by the Lake* for Ancient Faith Publishing. He holds degrees in psychology, philosophy, and education, as well as an MDiv from St. Vladimir's Seminary. He is a parishioner at All Saints Antiochian Orthodox Church in Chicago, Illinois.

We hope you have enjoyed and benefited from this book. Your financial support makes it possible to continue our nonprofit ministry both in print and online. Because the proceeds from our book sales only partially cover the costs of operating **Ancient Faith Publishing** and **Ancient Faith Radio**, we greatly appreciate the generosity of our readers and listeners. Donations are tax-deductible and can be made at **www.ancientfaith.com**.

To view our other publications,
please visit our website: **store.ancientfaith.com**

Bringing you Orthodox Christian music,
readings, prayers, teaching, and podcasts
24 hours a day since 2004 at
www.ancientfaith.com